American Corps of Engineers

Wooden Hull Inspection and Repair Manual

American Corps of Engineers

Wooden Hull Inspection and Repair Manual

ISBN/EAN: 9783954274277
Erscheinungsjahr: 2014
Erscheinungsort: Bremen, Deutschland

© maritimepress in Europäischer Hochschulverlag GmbH & Co. KG, Fahrenheitstr. 1, 28359 Bremen. Alle Rechte beim Verlag und bei den jeweiligen Lizenzgebern.

www.maritimepress.de | office@maritimepress.de

Bei diesem Titel handelt es sich um den Nachdruck eines historischen, lange vergriffenen Buches. Da elektronische Druckvorlagen für diese Titel nicht existieren, musste auf alte Vorlagen zurückgegriffen werden. Hieraus zwangsläufig resultierende Qualitätsverluste bitten wir zu entschuldigen.

American Corps of Engineers

Wooden Hull Inspection and Repair Manual

WOODEN HULL

INSPECTION & REPAIR MANUAL

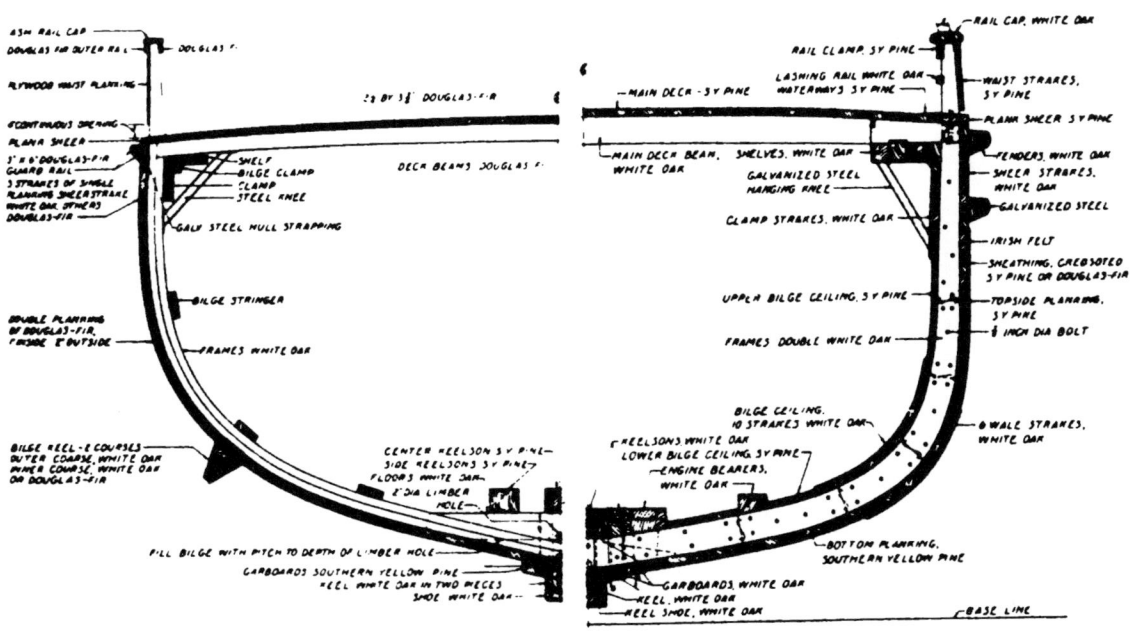

CONTENTS

		Page
I.	INTRODUCTION	1
II.	GUIDE TO INSPECTION	2
	A. General	2
	B. Hull Deficiencies	2
	C. Structural Problems	2
	D. Condition of Vessel for Inspection	2
	E. Visual Inspection	3
	F. Inspection for Decay and Marine Borers	3
	G. Inspection of Fastenings	5
	H. Inspection of Caulking	6
	I. Inspection of Fittings	6
	J. Hull Damage	6
	K. Deficiencies	7
III.	REPAIRS	8
	A. General	8
	B. Planking Repair and Notes on Joints	8
	C. Framing Repair	13
	D. Use of Fiberglass Reinforced Plastic	14
IV.	MATERIALS	14
	A. Wood	14
	B. Mechanical Fastenings	17
	C. Glues and Gluing	23
	D. Wood Preservatives	24
V.	DETERIORATION	28
	A. Decay	28
	B. Marine Borers	29
VI.	SKETCHES OF WOODEN CONSTRUCTION, ETC.	31
	A. Sketches	31
	B. Glossary	37
VII.	REFERENCES	43

ACKNOWLEDGMENT

The information contained herein relating to good practice in the inspection and repair of wooden vessels was originally prepared by the Merchant Marine Technical Division, Office of Merchant Marine Safety, U.S. Coast Guard, for Coast Guard Marine Inspectors, commercial marine surveyors, vessel owners and shipyards.

The information and suggestions were compiled from sources believed to be reliable, but correctness or completeness cannot be guaranteed.

I. INTRODUCTION

This publication has been prepared as a result of requests from the field for information concerning the inspection and repair of wooden hulls. These notes are intended as an aid to responsible persons in promoting uniformity in inspection procedures and in developing standards for their localities which reflect the overall concept of "good practice" with specific modifications dictated by local conditions. This information is furnished for guidance purposes. Where specifics are given, it should be understood that mandatory application is not necessarily intended. Nothing herein shall be taken as amending the applicable regulations, or as prescribing or limiting the authority and responsibility of the Officer in Charge, Marine Inspection, in the exercise of his good judgement.

It is expected these notes will require modification in the light of their use in the field. Comments and suggestions are welcome and revisions will be issued as necessary.

II. GUIDE TO INSPECTION

A. General

Intelligent inspection and repair of wooden construction requires knowledge and judgment. Inspection is made to determine that the vessel is safe and has a reasonable chance of remaining so until the next scheduled inspection. A good basic knowledge of wood construction and the deficiencies to which it is susceptible is essential.

B. Hull Deficiencies

Hull deficiencies in wooden vessels group themselves into three categories:

1. Time
   a. Decay
   b. Marine borers
   c. Electrolytic and Galvanic Action

2. Stress
   a. Cracks
   b. Broken members
   c. Failure of fastenings
   d. Failure of caulking

3. Damage
   a. Hull damage due to collision, grounding or to normal wear and tear

C. Structural Problems

In wooden vessels structural problems develop in nearly new vessels as well as in older ones. Deterioration, especially that caused by decay and marine borers, can occur with surprising rapidity. Boats which have been free of such infestations can become infected with slight changes in service area or operation. That the vessel was sound at its last inspection has less bearing on the present condition of a wooden vessel than on one of steel.

D. Condition of Vessel for Inspection

If practicable, inspect the vessel out of the water with the interior of the hull opened up as much as possible. The bilges and forepeak should be dry and reasonably clean and excess tackle, tools and gear which might interfere with proper inspection should be cleared away. This is not always possible. However hard to inspect (and thus hard to maintain) areas should not be missed.

Where the interior of the hull has closely fitted ceiling or paneling, sufficient access should be provided to allow examination of the interior at selected locations. Apparent soundness of the ceiling should not be taken as indicative of soundness beneath it.

E. <u>Visual Inspection</u>
An overall examination of the hull of a wooden vessel which has been in service can give the inspector an idea of the portions where deficiencies can be expected. Distorted planking, pulled butts, local damage and unexplained wetness or weeping are tell tale indications.

Particular attention should be paid to stern, transom, region under the covering boards, the wind and water area and around hull fittings. It is impossible to list each area of trouble in each type of boat. In general, areas which are hard to maintain, have poor ventilation or are subject to heavy stresses have the most deficiencies.

F. <u>Inspection for Decay and Marine Borers</u>
Serious deterioration of a wooden hull goes on within the wood itself with little or no outward sign until it is well advanced. In order to spot decayed (dry-rotted) wood, which has not progressed to the point where the wood appears eroded and spongy, sounding with a hammer can be of use. Unsound wood will give a dead or dull sound. Heavy timbers whose interiors are rotted may give a distinctive drum like tone. Where the sound is not that of good solid wood, the member is suspect. A probe or drill can then be used to determine the extent of decay.

It should be realized that decay progresses rapidly and that it is more economical to eliminate small decayed areas early than to become involved in costly major replacements caused by neglected decay.

It is imperative that indiscriminate probing and boring be avoided. Holes made by a probe or drill in the hull exterior are potential entry ways for marine borers. In the hull interior they allow easier moisture penetration and thus aid in starting decay.

Probing and boring should be done carefully and only where there is an indication from non destructive testing that the hull is unsound, not as a matter of routine.

Holes made by boring should be plugged with dowels or plugs which are glued in place, not merely driven into the wood. Plugs and dowels should preferably be treated with wood preservative to prevent future trouble. Areas which have been probed should be filled with a suitable compound. When covering boards or other obscuring construction is involved, it is often difficult to locate deteriorated members by probing. In such cases, when bolted or screwed fastenings are involved, check for tightness of randomly selected fastenings. If the member is solid, the fastening thus set up will take hold at the beginning of the turn. If serious decay is present the fastening will turn freely and fail to take a bite, indicating soft and spongy wood.

Decay (dry-rot) is most often found in the following locations:

1. In the wind and water area.

2. Around overboard discharges and other fittings.

3. In the stem area.

4. At the transom.

Internally

1. All areas that are poorly ventilated (especially the forepeak).

2. In the bilge especially at the turn and along the keel.

3. The lower courses of bulkhead planking.

4. Areas under refrigerators or other machinery which may drip fresh water.

5. In the area of butt blocks and longitudinal members where dirt and debris may have retained fresh water.

6. At the heads of frames caused by fresh water leakage through defective covering boards.

7. Where the futtocks of sawn frames join and at the faying surface where the frame abuts the hull planking.

8. At the terminal ends of frames, floors, engine foundations, etc. where end grain is present.

Under freezing temperature conditions wood structural members with a high moisture content, particularly in the bilge areas, may appear quite sound when, in fact, they may be in advanced stages of decay. Periodic examination of these areas should be conducted before freezing sets in or after allowing sufficient time for thawing.

The other principal form of deterioration which goes on within the wood is marine borer attack. Marine borers can attack any wood which is beneath the water. No species of wood is immune to attack and no method of protection of the wood is completely effective.

Borers can enter the wood through hairline breaks in sheathing (either copper or fiberglass) or through scrapes, nicks or tool marks in protective bottom paints. If borer infestation is suspected a spot check of the wood beneath the sheathing should be made.

A probe is the most effective tool to use in the detection of borers. Avoid over zealous probing since each probe hole is a potential site of borer entry. After probing is complete the resulting holes should be filled with a patching compound.

Marine Borers die when removed from the water for any period of time. A vessel which has been out of the water for a few days and is essentially dry will probably have no live borers.

Where borer attack is just starting it is possible to burn the holes clean with a torch and then fill them with a suitable compound. If the attack is extensive, however, the only method acceptable is to replace the affected wood.

The first principle in reducing the chance of borer attack is to keep the worm away from the wood. This is accomplished by sheathing or by toxic paints. If the protective coating is broken borers can enter. To prevent this sheathing, where fitted, should be unbroken and in good condition and the bottom paint should be free from scratches, nicks and scrapes before the vessel is again in the water.

Worm shoes, rubbing strakes and similar members whose protective coatings have been broken should be inspected carefully. If they have heavy borer infestation they should be replaced. Care should be taken to see that the infestation has not progressed from them to the main part of the hull structure. Though worm shoes are usually separated from the hull by creosote impregnated felt or by copper sheathing, this separation is usually not 100% effective.

G. Inspection of Fastenings

A boat is no better than its fastenings. Most hull fastenings are concealed from view, being countersunk and covered; their inspection is difficult.

Planking fastenings which are loose, broken or wasted often result in sprung butts or in planks which are loose or chatter when sounded with a hammer.

When fastenings are loose it does little permanent good to harden up those which exist. Additional fastenings, properly placed, are the preferred repairs where there is sufficient room to obtain good holding power without seriously weakening the planking. If there is not room, holes in the substructure from the old fastenings should be properly plugged and new fastenings of equivalent strength should be driven. Loose planking can also result from deteriorated frames and other sub-structure in which case refastening is useless unless the structure is first made sound.

Particular attention should be given exposed hull fittings and through bolts. These should be sounded with a hammer and, if suspect, some should be pulled for inspection. It is advisable to pry up on exposed bolt heads with a probe or screwdriver. Often the bolt will be completely wasted away in the middle, at the faying surface of the joint, and will come out when pried up. This is caused by moisture accumulation which, besides wasting the fastenings, forms an excellent place for decay to start.

H. Inspection of Caulking

Caulking is subject to deterioration. It is advisable to search the seams in any doubtful areas and re-caulk. Caulking should be uniform and well "horsed" home. This can be checked with an awl or a knife. Care should be taken that the caulking has not been driven clear through the seam. Over caulking is as bad as under caulking.

Extensive trouble with caulking is indicative of structural problems.

If a hull "works" excessively, the caulking will be squeezed out. In such cases, the hull structure will have to be made sound before caulking will hold.

In old hulls, where the seams have become enlarged from repeated re-caulking, copper or lead strips may have been nailed over the seams to act as caulking retainers. These are a temporary remedy and are an indication of poor general condition of the vessel. It is advisable that such strips be removed and the seams inspected for excessive width, poor caulking and decay. In some cases, wide seams or broken plank edges can be repaired by the use of thin graving pieces partially filling the wide seams. This procedure requires excellent workmanship and should be pursued with caution.

I. Inspection of Fittings

The rudder and the propeller struts and fastenings should be examined carefully. The steering arrangement should be inspected from the steering wheel to the heel pintle. Wear in the carrier bearing and excessive clearances elsewhere should be corrected. The tiller lines should be in good condition with shackles moused and bolts cottered.

The shaft log glands should be in good condition and the deadwood should be sound. This is often neglected and is a potential cause of leakage.

Propeller shaft cracks are sometimes found at the keyway. A careful examination here is essential. Magnetic particle testing is usually not available in a small boatyard so the inspector must depend on visually locating surface cracks. Dye penetrant testing is relatively inexpensive and can be useful when available.

J. Hull Damage

Most hull damage can be seen readily. Cracked and broken members are obvious faults.

Likely locations for cracks or breaks are in areas of high stress or where the structure undergoes a sudden change in shape. The turn of the bilge is the prime location for breakes of this type. The harder the bilge the more chance that damage has been done.

Wood hulls are more prone to secondary damage remote from the site of collision or grounding than are steel hulls. Damage may consist of sprung butts, pulled fastenings, sprung or cracked frames and misalignment of the structure. In inspecting any damaged wooden hull the entire vessel should be checked.

K. Deficiencies

When deficiencies are encountered an evaluation must be made to determine their extent and their effect on seaworthiness. The following factors must be weighed in making this determination:

1. Is the defect progressive and, if so, how can its progress be arrested?

2. How long will it be before the area in question is next inspected?

3. Is the work contemplated necessary to restore seaworthiness or to prevent the vessel from becoming unseaworthy, or is it a maintenance measure to prolong the life of the vessel?

Many deficiencies, particularly surface defects or scars caused by chafing, freezing and other forms of exterior deterioration are not as serious as they may first appear. Do not be hasty in requiring the correction of minor defects of this nature in otherwise sound seasoned planking.

Specific requirements detailing the nature and extent of required repairs should be written. However, with wooden vessels the general rule "renew as original" while applicable, is not always practical nor necessarily the best way to effect repairs. Most accepted methods of marine repair may be used as long as the vessel's strength is not reduced thereby.

Wood is a natural product; its quality cannot be controlled as closely as with a man-made product such as steel. Consequently the inspector should check the material to be used in the work. Special attention must be given the type of wood proposed for each purpose and the defects in each piece.

Requirements for adequate repairs are:

(1) Use of good material comparable in properties to that replaced.

(2) Repairs extensive enough to assure that the hull is essentially as strong as the existing original.

(3) Details and fastenings at least equivalent in strength and in quality to those replaced.

(4) Good workmanship.

III. REPAIRS

A. General

Wood boat construction varies widely from locality to locality and boat to boat. All types of repairs which an inspector may encounter cannot be listed. Representative types and standards which are given here are intended as a general guide to good practice and as an aid in evaluating required repairs. They are not rules which the responsible person must follow. Repair standards for wooden hulls should be developed for the locality on the basis of local conditions and practice.

B. Planking Repair and Notes on Joints

Fore and Aft Planking. When such planking is replaced, the frames and other structure should be thoroughly inspected and placed in good condition. Holes made by old fastenings should be properly plugged to insure that new fastenings will hold.

"Flats", "dutchmen" or short lengths of planking are normally not acceptable since they will not hold fastenings and are structurally unsound.

In boats with usual frame spacing the replacement plank should extend at least six frame spaces and no portion of a plank shorter than six frame spaces should be allowed to remain.

Where special conditions govern, this rule may be modified but, as a lower limit, the replacement plank should be at least 5 feet long and its butts should be spaced in accordance with the rule for butts in this chapter.

Fastenings should be at least equal in size and number to those of the rest of the planking.

When planking is placed on a boat, it should have the concave side of the annual rings facing toward the frame. This prevents "cupping" as the moisture content of the wood changes.

It is sometimes necessary to shape the inboard side of a replacement plank to fit tightly against the frames. The use of shims or packing pieces for this purpose should not ordinarily be allowed.

Diagonal Planking. The same principles apply to diagonal planking but due to the relatively short lengths of the individual planks a portion of a plank is seldom replaced.

BUTT BLOCKS

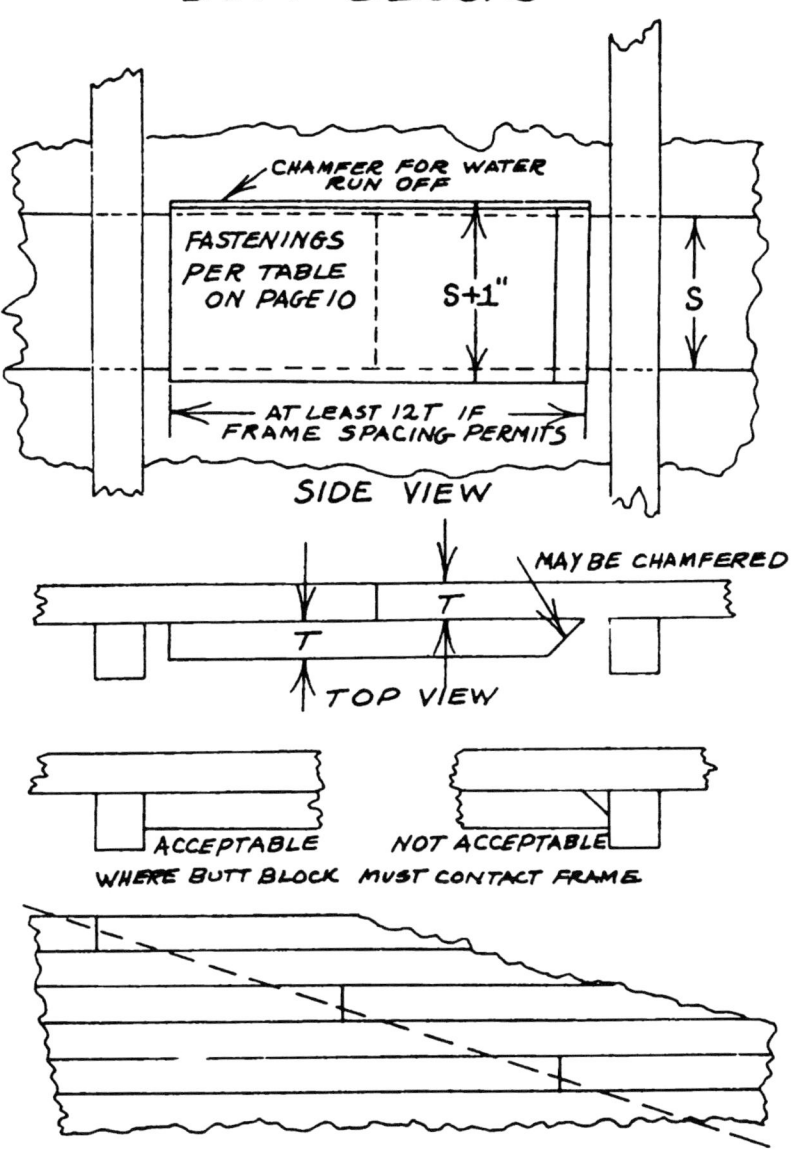

Because the proper repair of double diagonal planking is expensive and time consuming, short cuts involving the use of dutchmen and backing blocks are sometimes attempted. These should not be permitted. Most other planking systems follow the same basic principles of repair as outlined here. Good workmanship and care are the major requirements for proper repair.

Plywood Construction

In general, the replacement of a portion of a panel of plywood is not acceptable. However, in the case of a small damaged area between frames, a flush patch backed by a butt block may be used.

White lead or other suitable compound on the edges of the opening is an acceptable aid in sealing the patch. Calking should never be used and shims and fillers as a substitute for good workmanship are not acceptable. Care should be taken in allowing such a repair for small decayed areas since plywood has relatively low decay resistance. Once decay has started it travels rapidly in all directions.

Small surface defects may be repaired using commercial fillers (epoxy putty, etc.). In allowing this type of repair the wood must be decay free and all damaged wood removed. Quick repairs of this type are satisfactory where basic strength has not been affected. The danger lies in covering up progressive defects such as decay which grow worse under the repair material.

Butt Joints in Planking. Planking butts should not terminate on frames in normal construction. They should be located between frames on proper butt blocks, though in light construction with narrow strakes they may sometimes be found as glued scarf joints at the frames and in some construction with massive framing they may be found butted on the frames. As a rule of thumb, butts in adjacent planks should be at least three frame spaces apart. Those butts which fall in the same frame bay should be separated by at least three solid strakes. This is not always possible, especially at the end of the vessel, but serves to illustrate the principle of keeping butts separated as much as possible. Where frame spacing is unusual the following rule may be used as a guide.

Butts in adjacent strakes should be no closer together than 5 feet. If there is a solid strake between they should be no closer than 4 feet. Butts should be shifted so that three or more do not fall on a diagonal line.

To be effective a butt block must have adequate size. If the frame spacing allows, its length should be at least 12 times the planking thickness. Its thickness should be equal to the planking thickness and its width at least 1" greater than the strake width. Prior to installation it is recommended that the faying surface of block and strakes be coated with a wood preservative. The top of the butt block should be chamfered to allow for water run off. Avoid butting the block hard against the frames, if frame spacing permits, for the same reason.

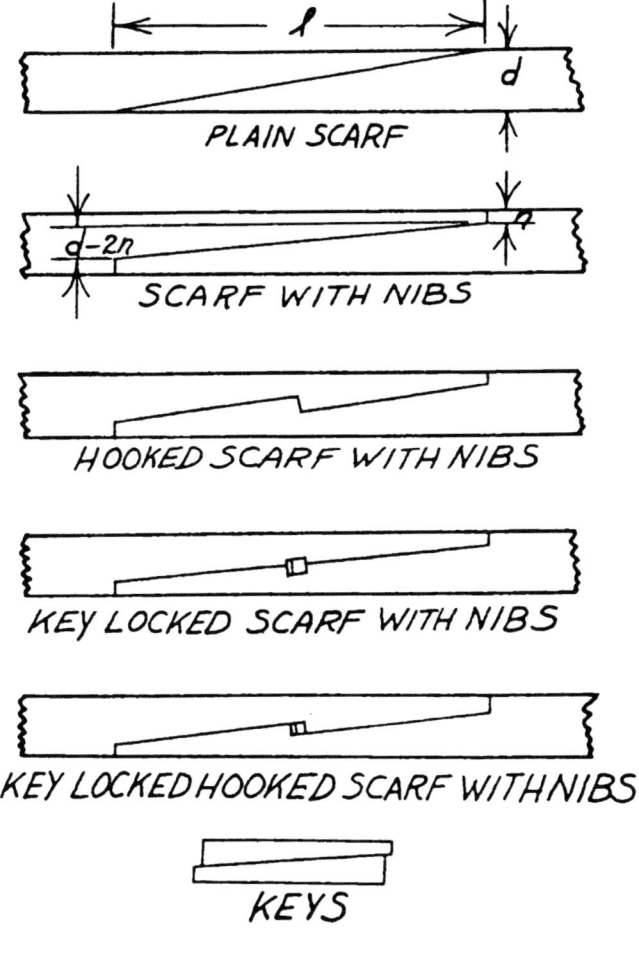

The fastenings of the strake to the butt block should be of equal strength to that of original butts. The fastening size should be equal or larger and no fewer number of fastenings should be allowed.

Plywood butt blocks may be used but it should be remembered that though plywood has greater uniformity of strength in all directions, it has somewhat less strength than the "along the grain" strength of the basic wood from which it is made.

For new construction or for repairs "not in kind" the following table lists the suggested number of fastenings for planking:

Suggested <u>Minimum</u> Number of Fastenings for Planking to Butts and Frames

Width of Plank (inches)	Number of Fastenings in Butt of <u>Each</u> plank	Number of Fastenings in Frame		
		½-1 Inch Plank Thickness	1-1½ Inch Plank Thickness	1½-2 Inch Plank Thickness
3-4	3	2	2	2
4-6	4	2*	2	2
6-7	5	3	2	2
7-8	5	3	3	2
8-10	6	3	3	3

*Planking at the side end of this range may require 3 fastenings.

<u>Glued Scarf Joints</u>. For a glued scarf joint the plain scarf without nibs is the simplest and strongest. Waterproof glue should be used and the slope of the joint should be 1/12 or flatter for maximum joint efficiency.

Scarf Slope (depth/length)	Typical Joint Efficiency for a well made glued joint without nibs
1/12	90%
1/10	85%
1/8	80%
1/5	65%

These efficiencies can be attained only with optimum gluing conditions and excellent workmanship.

<u>Mechanically Fastened Scarfs</u>. Mechanically fastened scarf joints are most often nibbed, hooked, or keyed to provide extra axial restraint and to aid watertightness.

The surface of the joint should be smooth and flat to insure good fit and watertightness.

The fastenings should be adequate in size and number and should be arranged so as to prevent splitting the wood.

The slope of the joint, $\frac{d-2n}{l}$, should be 1/12 or flatter.

Most mechanically fastened scarf joints are nibbed at the ends for a depth of approximately 25% of the depth of the member, giving a joint length of at least 6 times the depth.

A scarf joint which is fastened by mechanical means alone cannot, even under the best of conditions, produce a joint approaching a solid member in strength.

Glued Butt Joints. Glued butt joints never give joint efficiencies of over 20% and should not be permitted.

C. Framing Repair

Sister Frames. Damage to one or more scattered or isolated frames can be repaired by the use of sister frames though it is preferred that the frame be replaced if practicable. Damage to more than two adjacent frames should not be repaired with sister frames.

The preferred type of sister frame is one of equal or greater size than the damaged one and as long as possible. This frame should be fastened to the planking and other structure with fastenings at least equal in size and number to those of the damaged member. In placing the frame adequate wood preservative on all faying surfaces is recommended.

Long sister frames, well tied in to the main structure of the vessel should not normally butt against damaged frames though this is acceptable where it forms the best method of tying in the new frame. If the frames abutt, a good sealer is required to exclude moisture from between the pieces.

Where structural or machinery interference or other reasons prevent the fitting of a long sister frame, well tied into the other structure, a shorter "partial sister" may be fitted as a temporary repair. This should extend as far as is practicable on both sides of the damage and should be securely fastened to the damaged frame by through bolting or equivalent means as well as to the planking and other structure. Provisions should be made to exclude moisture from between the pieces.

A good wood preservative is recommended for use on all faying surfaces. Assure that precautions are taken that standing water cannot accumulate at the top of the partial frame and cause decay. A sister frame should not be used as a repair for decayed frames. The decayed wood will eventually "seed"

the sound wood with decay spores in spite of any attempts to prevent it by
the use of wood preservatives or to isolate the new wood with sealing compounds.
When extensive decay is present in a frame the only permanent repair is to
replace it and any adjacent wood affected.

   Decayed Frame Heads. Heads of frames under the covering boards often
become decayed. With sawn frames, this can be corrected by replacing the
upper futtock. If the futtock is long or the frame is in one piece, it can
often be cropped off well below the rot (at least 2 feet is a good rule)
and a piece spliced in using a glued and screwed scarf joint of proper dimensions.
As an alternate measure a lap joint of sufficient length may replace the scarf.
Repairs to more than two adjacent damaged frame heads should not be made by
short cropping but should be made by renewing the frames or replacing the damaged
sections by scarfing and then sistering the frame.

D. Use of Fiberglass Reinforced Plastic. Glassing an unsound structure as
a way of restoring strength is a temporary repair. This is especially true
of glassing planking or other areas which tend to work or "come and go".
The laminate has little flexibility along its length and breadth and tends
to develop "tension cracks" which destroy watertightness and strength.

   Before allowing any wooden structure to be repaired using reinforced
resin, an evaluation should be made considering the following items in
addition to those noted before.

   (1) In the hull, even a hairline crack can allow undetected
       entry of marine borers.

   (2) With old structure which has been painted or preserved a
       good bond is very difficult to attain.

   (3) Any rot present may continue to grow worse under the glass
       if the proper conditions of moisture and heat develop.

   (4) It is difficult to acquire enough strength from a reinforced
       resin coating to make up that lost from the unsound substructure.

   (5) It is difficult to check the soundness of the substructure
       once the glass has been applied.

   Full Sheathing of an existing wooden hull with fiberglass reinforced
plastic as a method of restoring strength and watertightness to a deteriorated
vessel is not normally acceptable.

IV. MATERIALS
   A. Wood
       The best single source of information available in the broad field
of wood technology is "The Wood Handbook" (Handbook No. 72) developed

by the Forest Products Laboratory of the Department of Agriculture. This book can be obtained from the Superintendent of Documents, Washington 25, D. C. It is highly recommended as a thoroughly practical work which should be part of the technical library of every inspection office and every wood boat building or repair yard.

<u>Shipbuilding Wood</u>. Douglas fir, southern yellow pine (long leaf), and white oak furnish over one half of the wood used for boat and shipbuilding. Choice of various species depends upon their properties, availability and cost.

Where requirements call for strength, moderate to good decay resistance and ability to hold fastenings well (frames, keels, stems, etc.), the following wood are most commonly used:

        Douglas fir
        Southern yellow pine (long leaf)
        Teak
        Western Larch
        White Oak

Where light wood which is easy to work and is warp and decay resistant is required (planking, etc.) the following woods are most commonly used:

        Alaska cedar
        Cypress
        Mahogany
        Cedar (Port Orford, Northern White, and Western Red)
        Red wood
        Tangile (Philippine hardwood)

Where light, easily worked and strong woods of moderate to low decay resistance are required, the following woods have found favor:

        Sitka Spruce
        Western hemlock
        White pine
        Yellow Poplar

There are many other varieties suitable for boat use. These are listed together with their properties in the Wood Handbook and in Volume 1 of Bureau of Ships Publication "Wood - A Manual for its Use As A Shipbuilding Material".

<u>Bending Woods</u>. Unseasoned white oak is the choice bending wood. It bends readily and is high in decay resistance. Red oak, hickory, rock elm, white ash, beech, birch, and hard maple, also bend readily but do not have the decay resistance of white oak. White oak and its best substitute, rock elm, are expensive and hard to obtain, but do the best job.

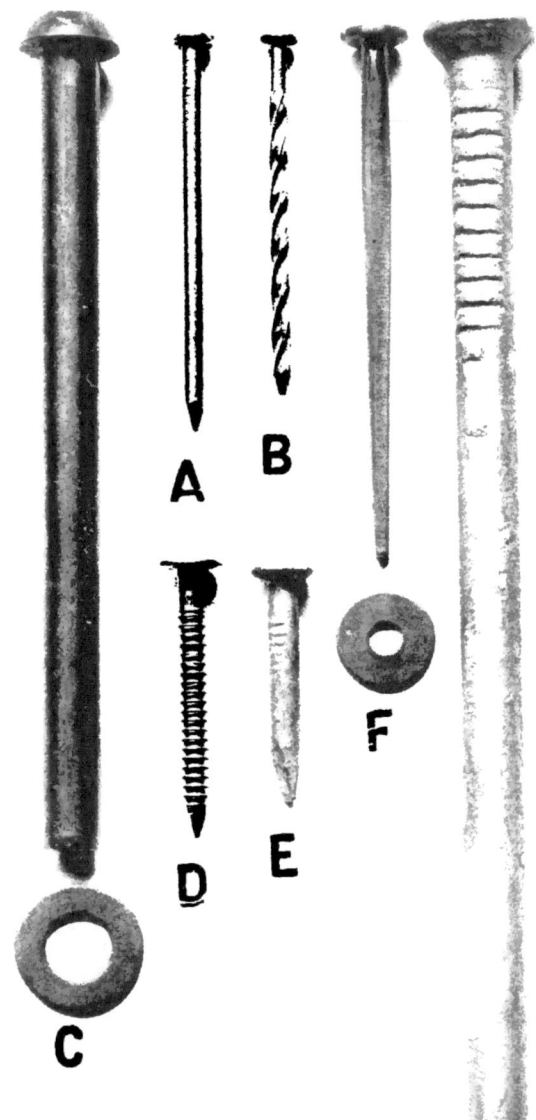

A- Wire nail. (not commonly used in boat construction)
B- Spiral grooved nail.
C- Drift bolt.
D- Boat nail with grooved shank.
E- Chisel point boat nail.
F- Square cut boat nail with rivet burr and cut washer.
G- Boat spike with chisel point.

Wood Defects. Wood, being a natural material, is not uniform in quality and is subject to defects. Some of these affect only the appearance of the wood. Others affect the strength of the wood and are of importance.

The chapter of "The Wood Handbook" on Stress Grades and Working Stresses discussed defects of interest to persons concerned. Among the most important of these are -

Knots, Shakes, Checks, Splits and Pitch Pockets.

Plywood. Plywood is a built up board of laminated veneers in which the grain of each "ply" is perpendicular to the ones adjacent to it. Its chief advantages lie in more nearly equal strength properties along the length and width of the panel, resistance to change in dimensions with moisture content and resistance to splitting. Major disadvantages are low decay resistance and the difficulty of painting it properly.

Plywood is excellent where strength is needed in more than one direction and where the relatively large size of the panels available can be utilized. It is no stronger than the wood from which it is made and is not a cure-all for wood structural problems.

Plywood is made from several types of wood and in many different types and grades. In general, "Marine-Exterior" type of fir plywood or its equivalent, technical or Type 1 hardwoods are the only plywoods acceptable for use as hull planking. These plywoods are identical with ordinary "Exterior" type in that they are bonded with waterproof glue by a process using heat and pressure. Their advantage lies in the fact that the interior plies contain few gaps and thus its strength, ability to hold fastenings and resistance to decay are much higher than "Exterior". "Marine" plywood is more expensive than "Exterior" but provides additional safety and durability.

Fir plywood is graded according to the appearance of the exterior veneers. These grades run from grade "N" intended for natural finish and grade "A", suitable for painting, down through grade "D", the poorest quality. Each side is graded. For example, a panel may be graded "Marine Exterior A-B" where "Marine Exterior" refers to the type of bonding used and the allowable defects in the inner plies, while "A-B" refers to the appearance of the two sides of the panel.

Marine plywood is usually available only in appearance grades B-B and better. The strength of the wood is indirectly reflected in the grading since the poorer grades have openings, splits, pitch pockets and other defects which adversely affect strength and decay resistance.

All plywood is marked with its classification. This classification may appear on the panel back, on its edge or both.

B. Mechanical Fastenings

Mechanical fastenings should be of material suitable for the service intended. Ferrous fastenings should be hot-dipped galvanized. Among the usual non-ferrous types brass is not acceptable where it will be exposed to salt water attack.

Caution should be used in selecting fastening material because of the problem of galvanic action which can arise if dissimilar metals are used close to one another. A bronze washer used with a steel bolt will result in the eating away of the steel.

GALVANIC SERIES IN SEA WATER

PROTECTED END (CATHODIC OR MOST NOBLE)
Monel
Copper
Red Brass
Aluminum Brass
Yellow Brass - Silicon Bronze
Nickel - Inconel
Naval Brass
Muntz Metal - Manganese Bronze
Lead - Tin
Stainless Steel (Reference should be made to the specifications for stainless steels being considered since they vary widely in their properties)
50-50 Lead-Tin Solder
13% Cr Stainless Steel
Cast Iron
Mild Steel - Wrought Iron
Aluminum - Cadmium
Galvanized Steel
Zinc
Magnesium
CORRODED END (ANODIC OR LEAST NOBLE)

The number, size and spacing of fastenings should be equivalent to or better than those replaced. For new construction and for repairs "not in kind" a general guide for good practice is the "National Design Specifications for Stress Grade Lumber and its Fastenings", a publication of the National Lumber Manufacturers Association. In applying the standards found therein, consideration should be given to the severe conditions of marine service.

A general guide for use of the various types of fastenings follows:

Bolts. Bolt holes should be of such diameter as to provide an easy fit without excessive clearance. Tight fit requiring forcible driving of the bolt is not recommended.

Washers. A washer not less than a standard cut washer or, in lieu thereof, a metal plate or strap should be inserted between the bolt head and the wood and between the wood and the nut.

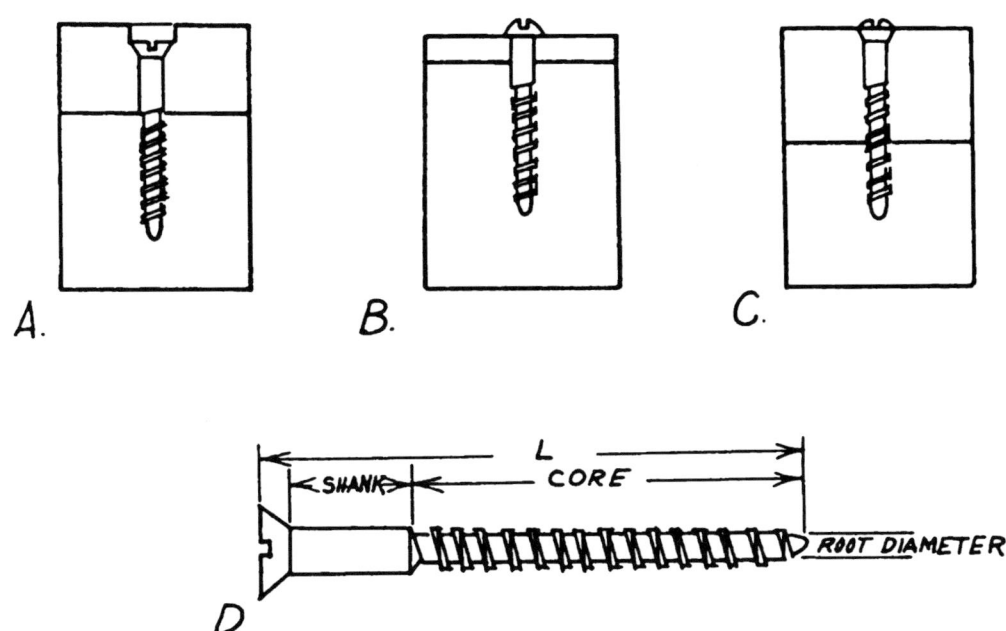

TYPES OF WOOD SCREWS
A. FLAT-HEAD, B. ROUND-HEAD, C. OVAL-HEAD
A SHOWS A SCREW PROPERLY INSERTED AND COUNTERSUNK.
B AND C SHOW INCORRECTLY INSERTED SCREWS.
D SHOWS PRINCIPAL PARTS OF A WOOD SCREW.

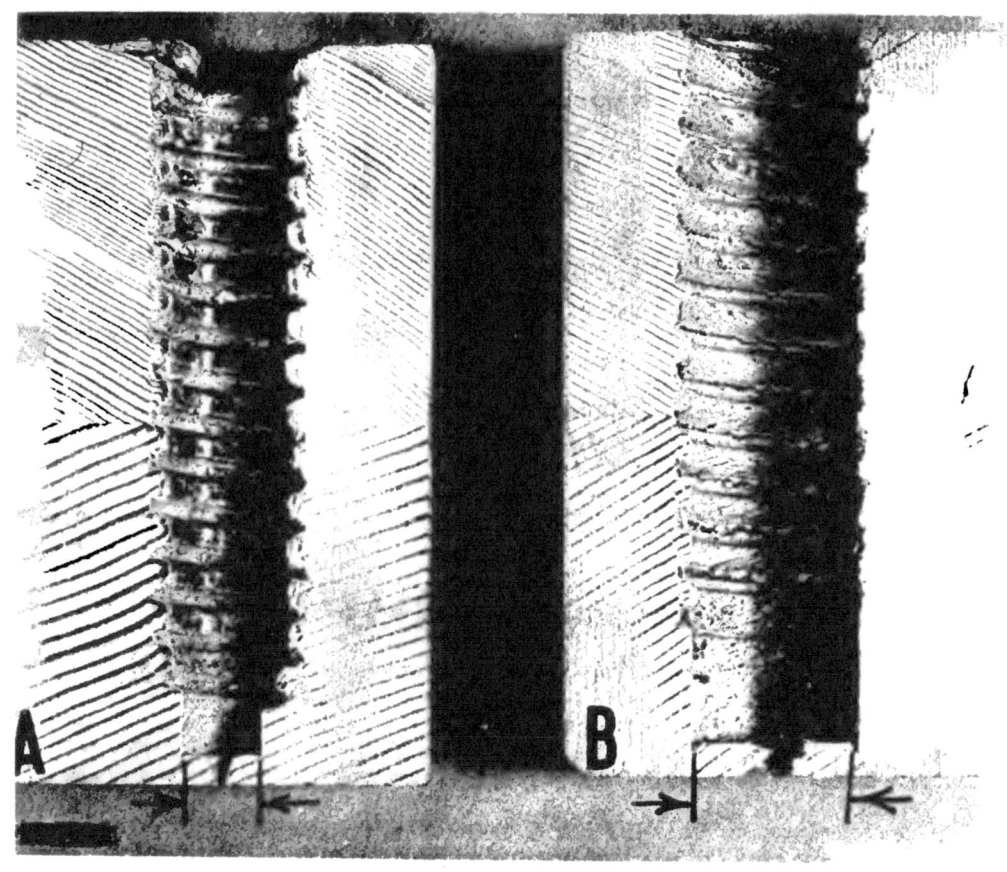

SECTIONS THROUGH SCREW HOLES

A- Proper lead hole size.
B- Lead hole too large. Screw drove easily but had poor holding power.

Stopwater. A suitable wicking or stopwater should be fitted in way of the faying surface of the joint at each through bolt subject to moisture.

Placement of Bolts in Joint. The center to center distance between bolts in a row should be not less than four times the bolt diameter.

The spacing between rows of bolts should be 5 times the bolt diameter for a bolt whose length from the bottom of the head to the inner side of the nut when tightened is 6 times the bolt diameter or longer. For short bolts, this distance may be decreased but in no case should be less than 3 times the bolt diameter.

The "end distance" from the end of a bolted timber to the center of the bolt hole nearest the end should be at least 7 times the bolt diameter for softwoods and at least 5 times the bolt diameter for hardwoods.

The "edge distance" from the edge of the member to the center of the nearest bolt hole should be at least $1\frac{1}{2}$ times the bolt diameter. For bolts whose length is over six times their diameter use one half the distance between bolt rows and in no case below $1\frac{1}{2}$ times the bolt diameter.

For perpendicular to the grain loadings (joints at right angles), the edge distance toward which the load acts, should be at least 4 times the bolt diameter.

Bolting Groups. In general, all groups of bolts should be symmetrical in the members. The individual fastenings should be offset slightly as necessary to avoid placing more than one on the same grain.

Screwed Fastenings.
Lead Holes. Lead holes for wood screws should be about 90% of the root diameter of the screw for hardwoods and about 70% of the root diameter for softwoods. For large screws and for hardwoods, a shank hole of a diameter equal to the shank of the screw and of a depth equal to the shank may be used to facilitate driving. Lag screws should always have a shank hole.

The lead hole for the threaded portion of a lag screw should have a diameter of 65-85% of the shank diameter in oak and 60-75% in douglas fir and southern pine with a length equal to the length of the threaded portion. Denser woods require larger lead holes and the less dense require smaller holes. For long screws or for screws of large diameter, lead holes slightly larger than those recommended here should be used. The threaded portion of the screw should be inserted by turning and not by driving with a hammer.

Lubricants. Suitable lubricants should be used on screws, expecially in dense wood, to make insertion easier and prevent damage to the screw.

Depth. Penetration of the threaded portion for at least a distance of 7 screw diameters for hardwoods and 10-12 times in softwoods is required for maximum holding power.

Glue line too thick. Caused by
too long an assembly period.

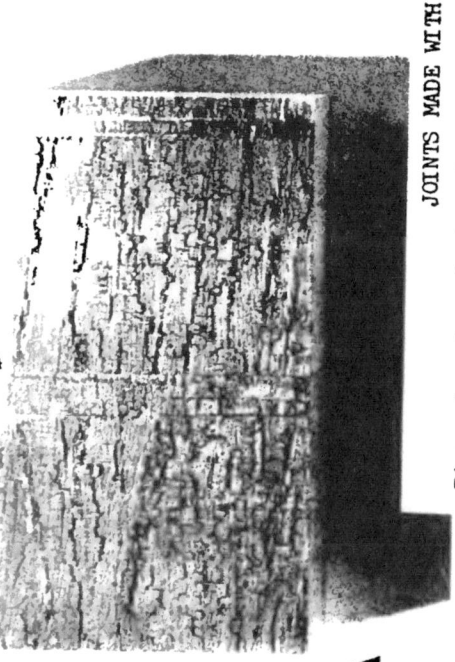

A

Glue line too thin. Caused by
too short an assembly period.

B

JOINTS MADE WITH RESORCINAL GLUE

Pieces have been broken along the joint. The broken pieces lie side by side.

Joint broken before glue has cured
completely. This can happen if clamps
are removed too soon.

C

Well made joint. Note the high percentage
of failure that took place in the wood
clear of the glue line.

D

Loading. If possible, screws should be placed so that they are loaded across the screw and not in withdrawal.

The spacing, end distance and edge distances for wood screws should be such as to prevent splitting the wood. Lag screws should follow the rules for bolts.

Nails and Spikes. Cut nails have relatively poor holding power in joints which are subject to moisture changes. Their use in marine applications should be avoided. Barbed nails are better suited for marine service.

Lead Holes. Lead holes for nailed joints may be 3/4 of the diameter of the nail without causing loss of strength.

Types of Load. If possible, nails should be loaded across the nail and not in the direction of withdrawal. This is especially important in end grain.

Spacing of Nails. The end and edge distances and spacings of the nails should be such as to prevent splitting of the wood.

Boat Spikes and Drift Bolts
Lead Holes. Lead holes for boat spikes should be the size of the short dimension of the spike and should extend approximately 75% of the spike depth. The lead holes for drift bolts should be slightly less than the bolt diameter and of a depth equal to the bolt length.

Type of Load. Where possible, spikes and drift bolts should not be loaded in withdrawal. This is especially important in end grain.

Insertion. A clinch ring or washer may be used under the head to prevent crushing of the wood. Spikes should be driven with the edge of the chisel point across the grain to avoid splitting the wood.

Spacing of Spikes and Drift Bolts. The end distance, edge distance and spacing of the spikes should be such as to avoid splitting the wood.

C. Glues and Gluing
Modern glues of the resorcinol and phenol-resorcinol resin types are the most satisfactory for severe service use such as for marine repair. Other glues have lower resistance to moisture and should be avoided where this is an important factor.

Not all wood are easily glued. Wet wood (above about 15% moisture content) is difficult to glue as is very dry wood. Normal seasoned wood of most species can be glued. Strong glued joints are possible only using the side grain of wood. These joints can be very nearly as strong as the wood itself. It is impossible to join end grain with glue and get joints which are even 20% as strong as the wood. A scarf or some other form of joint which gives a surface approaching side grain condition must be used where end connection is desired.

The glue manufacturer's instructions must be followed. Curing temperature and surface condition are important. The temperature must be about 70°F or higher for a full cure of resorcinol resin glue and the surface should be smooth. In the past, surfaces have been intentionally roughened in the mistaken belief that slightly rough surfaces glue better. This is not true. Waterproof glues are poor fillers. Thus the surfaces should be as smooth as possible.

D. Wood Preservatives

The use of wood preservatives is not required. However, their use in wood under severe service conditions will pay for itself many times in decreased decay and borer attack and thus decreased repair and replacement costs. Their proper use should be encouraged since it increases the chance of the vessel remaining sound until her next inspection and thus contributes to maintaining a reasonable standard of safety.

Wood preservatives used for protection against decay fungi and marine borers either kill the organism or prevent it from growing. For marine use the preservative must offer no toxic hazard to the crew, must be free from objectionable odors and must be able to remain in the wood and do its work in the presence of moisture. No known wood preservative is ideal for marine use but certain ones have proved effective for specific applications.

There are two general classes of wood preservatives, oil soluble and water soluble. Both have been used in the marine industry.

Oil Soluble Preservatives

Coal Tar Creosote. One of the most used of the oil soluble preservatives is coal tar creosote. This preservative is highly toxic to wood attacking organisms, is relatively insoluble in water and is easy to apply. It has some disadvantages, however, which limit its use in the marine field. It has a distinctive unpleasant odor, is somewhat of a fire hazard when freshly applied and causes skin irritation in some individuals. Its main disadvantage is that it is almost impossible to make paint or other coatings adhere to it.

Copper Naphthanate Solutions. Copper napthanate solutions form one of the most used groups of marine wood preservatives. A three percent solution, equivalent to one half of one percent copper by weight, provides good protection against decay when properly applied. The protection afforded against marine borers is slight. Wood treated with copper naphthanate is a distinctive green color. Much of the "treated wood" which can be purchased is preserved with copper naphthanate. The paintability, glue bonding ability, and structural stability of the wood is only slightly affected by the copper salts. These properties will vary, however, depending upon the oil used as a solvent.

Pentachlorophenol Solutions. "Penta" solutions have proven satisfactory for marine use. Field tests have shown that a 5% solution offers adequate protection against decay when proper application techniques are used. Little if any protection against marine borers is provided.

Pentachlorophenol does not give wood any distinctive color. In itself, it affects the characteristics of wood very little. The final effect of the preservation treatment on physical characteristics depends upon the petroleum solvent used.

Water Repellent Preservatives. Copper naphthanate and "penta" are often combined with water repellents. These repellents aid in stabilizing the moisture content of the treated wood. This is a material aid in reducing the chance that decay growth conditions will occur. In order to be effective these solutions should contain no less than 5% pentachlorophenol or 2% copper in the form of copper naphthanate.

Solvents. Almost any petroleum product from mineral spirit to used engine oil can be used as a vehicle for the preservative depending upon local conditions. In general, the heavier high viscosity residium types offer the best retention. The choice of solvent is usually a compromise of effectiveness, paintability and initial cost.

Water Preservatives. Waterborne preservatives include zinc chloride, tanalith, copper arsenite, chromated zinc arsenate and many others. Their major applications are those in which the leeching out of the preservative by moisture is not a problem. In general, these preservatives have not proven satisfactory for severe marine service. Some preserved wood obtained for repair use may have been pressure treated with one of these preservatives. It can give satisfactory service if care is taken to use it in a location where it is protected from the action of rain and sea water.

Methods of Treatment
Pressure Treatment. In the commercial treating of wood a method utilizing high pressure is often used. This method requires expensive equipment and is seldom seen in a boat yard. Nonpressure treatments available to the boat yard are brushing, cold soaking and various types of "hot and cold" bath processes.

Brush Treatment. The simplest way of applying a preservative solution is to brush it on. Every crack and check must be flooded with preservative if the treatment is to be effective. Small pieces such as butt blocks can be dipped into the preservative. Solutions of pentachlorophenol or copper naphthanate, available commercially, have proved effective when used in this way.

"Penta" stock solutions are available in what is known as 1:5 and 1:10 strengths, (i.e. the solution must be diluted one part of solution to five or ten parts of solvent to achieve a "normal" wood preserving solution.) These stock solutions are used without dilution for preserving cracks, holes resulting from old fastenings, for coating joints and hard to get spots, etc. Care must be exercised since wood preservatives are toxic. When using the brush-on method the entire surface must be thoroughly coated.

Soaking. Cold soaking in copper naphthanate or "penta" solutions for periods of up to 48 hours provides much better retention of the preservative than does a brushing. An even better method consists of heating the wood in a hot preservative bath and then transferring it to a cold bath of preservative. The heating causes the air entrapped in the wood to expand. The sudden cooling sets up a vacuum which aids preservative penetration.

The effectiveness of a preserving treatment depends on the amount of preservative which is retained in the wood. This is often difficult to determine. Requirements in Federal Specification TT-W-571 for recommended net retentions of oil borne preservatives are shown in the following table. This amount will provide good protection and even lesser amounts will still offer a considerable measure of protection.

Recommended Net Retentions of Preservative

Service	Coal Tar Creosote	Product Pentachloro- phenol 5% - Petroleum Oil	Copper Naphthanate (0.75% cer metal) in petroleum oil
Lumber and Structural Timber			
In Contact with Ground or water	14 - 20 lb/cu ft	10 lb/cu ft	10 lb/cu ft
Not in Contact with Ground or Water	6 lb/cu ft	6 lb/cu ft	6 lb/cu ft

Treating Isolated Decay

A method which can arrest the progress of incipient decay, at least temporarily, is as follows:

> The affected area is scraped clear of all decayed material and for some distance into apparently clear sound wood. A strong preservative solution, for example 1:10 pentachloro-phenol stock solution, is applied freely. This is allowed to soak in and dry. Repeated applications are made until the wood refused to take any more preservative. Often a small "cofferdam" can be made to retain a pool of preservative over the area. To be effective the preservative must sink in and sterilize the wood for a considerable distance since decay sends out spores ahead of the damaged area.

After the treatment is completed the cavity made by the scraping may be left unfilled but it should be properly painted. Filling it will simply hide any additional rot still working.

This method is a temporary repair only. It usually will slow decay atta but will seldom eliminate all traces of decay.

"Salting" and Other Bilge Water Treatment

Decay will grow in a boat only where fresh water is present. This may be in the form of condensation or may come from rain, fresh water drains, or other sources. Salt water will not support fungus growth. The fungus usually does not die but its attack slows or stops.

In some areas of the country, it has been the practice to "salt" the bilges with rock salt. There are two disadvantages to this practice.

1. The salt dissolves readily and must be replaced often. A large part of it goes over the side when the bilges are pumped.

2. Strong salt solutions are hard on fastenings and metal parts. The wood stays sound but the life of the metal parts is reduced.

For these reasons, "salting" is of doubtful value.

Extensive tests have been run[1] on various chemicals to replace rock salt. The ones that offer the best promise are pentachlorophenol or orthophenylphenol. These chemicals, normally thought of as insoluble in water can be applied in the following manner:

Nylon "bean bags" containing crystalline "penta" are made and distributed through the bilge. A number of very small ones is superior to a few larger ones. Care must be taken in handling the "penta" since, like all good fungicides, it is toxic.

The "penta" goes into solution in the bilge water. This is very slight (about 20 parts per million) so that in spite of frequent pumping, very little penta is used up. The slight amount of penta dissolved makes the water fungistatic, that is to say, it will not support fungus growth. As long as the bean bags remain a considerable amount of decay protection is afforded. The solution is harmless to fastenings and metal parts and, with normal precaution, is not hazardous to handle. Since very little penta is used the cost of the treatment is surprisingly low.

In his conclusion, Dr. Scheffer states "Judging from these results, bilge water saturated with orthophenylphenol or with pentachlorophenol might be expected to preserve any wood that is wetted by it frequently and exclusively".

Caulking. The art of caulking is an ancient one which requires experience and a certain "touch". A good caulker makes his work look easy but it is a skill which takes much experience to develop.

---

[1] Scheffer, T. G., _Treatment of Bilge Water to Control Decay in the Bilge Area of Wooden Boats._ Journal of the Forest Products Research Society, Madison, Wisconsin: September, 1959.

Boats are caulked with caulking cotton, oakum is used for large vessels. Caulking cotton comes in bundles which can be shredded out to proper size for the seam. Plumber's caulking stuff which is short stranded should never be used. The caulking stuff is driven into the seam with a caulking iron forming loops with each drive of the iron. These loops should touch each other when in place. After the caulking is in place it is redriven or horsed home with the iron leaving room for filling the seam. Various irons of different shapes are used depending upon the location and condition of the seam.

Caulking should never be driven through the seam but should be in a "rope" about half way through. Caulking may be driven dry but it will not last as long as that which has been lubricated with linseed oil or other suitable lubricant. After caulking the seam may be filled with seam compound, white lead putty or other material as the circumstances require. Old caulking should be "reefed out" prior to putting in new. If the seams are narrow they are often opened up with a "dump iron" or a reaming iron to facilitate caulking.

In older vessels the seams may have been widened by repeated caulking over the years. This condition, coupled with unsound frames and structure, may make it impossible to keep caulking in the seams. Some owners may have fastened strips of lead or copper over the seams in an effort to correct the trouble. This "stop gap" method does little to maintain watertightness and may cover up deterioration. The preferred method of repair is to strengthen the structure and the fastenings prior to recaulking. If this does not stop the trouble portions of the boat may require replanking.

V. DETERIORATION
A. Decay

Wood has proved itself to be good for long service under proper conditions. One of the greatest enemies of wood is decay or "rot". Much of this rot in boats is preventable if care is used in construction, maintenance and repair.

Decay in wood is caused by various fungi which are living organisms whose growth depends upon suitable temperature ($50°$ to $90°F$), suitable food (wood) and moisture. Wood that is dry will not rot nor will waterlogged wood. In order to provide a condition suitable for fungus growth wood must be moist (from 20 to 30% moisture content). This condition is promoted by poor ventilation. A well designed vessel should have adequate ventilation of its enclosed spaces. Bilges, cabins etc., of vessels in service should be opened periodically to allow a change of air. Good ventilation of interior structure in wooden hulls is one of the most effective measures in the prevention of decay.

Not all wood offers the same natural resistance to decay. Most wood species have moderate to low natural decay resistance. In general, heartwood is much more decay resistant than sapwood of the same species.

The fresh surface of decay is usually fluffy or cottony as contrasted to the powdery growth of mold. The various rot fungi act in slightly different ways but is left unchecked all can destroy the wood in short order.

It is relatively easy to recognize advanced decay. The wood is discolored, softened and brittle and may show cracks and collapsed areas. Early decay is more difficult to recognize. It may appear as a discoloration in streaks along the grain of the wood. No known test available to the inspector can be substituted for experience in spotting early decay. The mere presence of a stain does not indicate decay. Wood is prone to pick up stain and coloration from blood, fish, bird droppings and various other sources. Probing with an ice pick is sometimes a help in finding "soft spots" in areas in which visual inspection and sounding with a hammer have aroused suspicion as to the soundness of the wood. Turning up a splinter with a knife blade may also help. Sound wood tends to produce long clean splinters while wood with early decay, having lost much of its strength, will break off abruptly.

While the final test for rot is to collect samples from the interior of the wood by probing, as noted above, or by boring with a drill these procedures should be used with caution. <u>Excessive drilling and probing can weaken otherwise sound structure.</u>

Fungi are living plants that can and do travel from an infected area to a sound one. It is useless to place sound wood against rotten and expect the sound wood to survive.

Once decay is well started in a piece it is difficult and most often impossible to stop its progress. In early decay the use of wood preservatives can be of aid in controlling the attack. Used properly in new construction or in repair they can prevent it.

B. Marine Borers

Marine borers are present to a varying degree in almost all the salt and brackish waters of the world. They attack practically every species of wood used in boat construction. There is no sure method of protection from their attack. The two principal methods are to physically keep the worm away from the wood (sheathing) and to make the wood unattractive to the worm (toxic substances and coatings). The main types of marine borers are listed in the following paragraphs.

Shipworms. These pests are actually mollusks and not worms. There are several species of Teredo and Bankia in this group. Though they vary in detail, their attack upon wood follows the same pattern.

They start their lives as tiny free swimmers. Upon finding a suitable home, even a tiny crack in a sheathed bottom, they attach themselves and quickly change form. As a pair of cutting shells develop on their heads they bury themselves in the wood and feed upon it. Their tails or "syphons" always remain at the entrance to their burrow but, as the worms grow, their heads eat channels in the wood. The entrance holes always remain small and hardly noticeable but the interior of the wood becomes honeycombed. When they are not crowded some species of shipworm can grow to lengths exceeding four feet.

Martesia. These are wood boring mollusks which resemble small clams like the shipworm, they enter the wood when they are small and do their damage within. They do not grow to the length of shipworms but, nevertheless, they can do considerable damage. Their main area is in the Gulf of Mexico.

Limnoria and Sphaeroma. These are small creatures which attack the surface of the wood. When large numbers of them are present the surface can be eaten away to such an extent that the remaining sound wood between their burrows can be removed by the action of moving water. This erosion causes the pests to burrow deeper. Their attack, though serious, is much more easily detected than that of shipworms.

Protecting Wood Hulls from Marine Borers. Coal tar creosote is the most effective chemical for use against marine borers. However, it adds considerably to hull weight, has an objectionable odor and does not allow the effective application of antifouling paints. Wood which has been treated with certain other wood preservatives has some resistance to borer attack while an unbroken layer of copper bottom paint or of sheathing prevents the entry of the borer.

Any break in the protective coating is an open invitation to borer infestation. It is of first importance that the bottom coating of a boat be continuous. Tool marks, scrapes, nicks, etc., should be properly preserved and painted prior to refloating the vessel.

The same principle applies to bottom sheathing whether copper or fiberglass reinforced resin. A small break can admit enough shipworms to honeycomb the structure of the ship while the sheathing makes their detection difficult. In order to protect the hull coatings, some boats are fitted with worm shoes attached to the bottom of the keel and separated from it by creosote soaked felt or copper sheathing. These shoes are designed to take the scraping of any grounding, to have their protective coating broken rather than that of the hull and thus protect it from worm attack. All such shoes, rubbing strakes, etc., should be viewed with suspicion since it is impossible to assure 100% separation from the hull and since an infected worm shoe is a source of "free swimmers" which can move to any break in the protective coating of the hull.

Metal shoes and rubbing pieces are sometimes fitted for the same purpose. Of course these never become worm infested but they must be carefully fitted and bedded to prevent borers from working their way underneath the shoe around the edges and thus into the main structure.

VI. SKETCHES OF WOODEN CONSTRUCTION AND A SHORT GLOSSARY ON WOOD AND WOODEN VESSELS

   A. SKETCHES

   Plate 1-Framing for Wooden Boats (Sections)
   Plate 2-Sections Typical of Heavy Construction
   Plate 3-Typical Heavy Stem Construction
   Plate 4-Typical Heavy Stern Construction
   Plate 5-Stopwaters in a Stem Piece

TYPICAL FRAMING (SECTIONS)

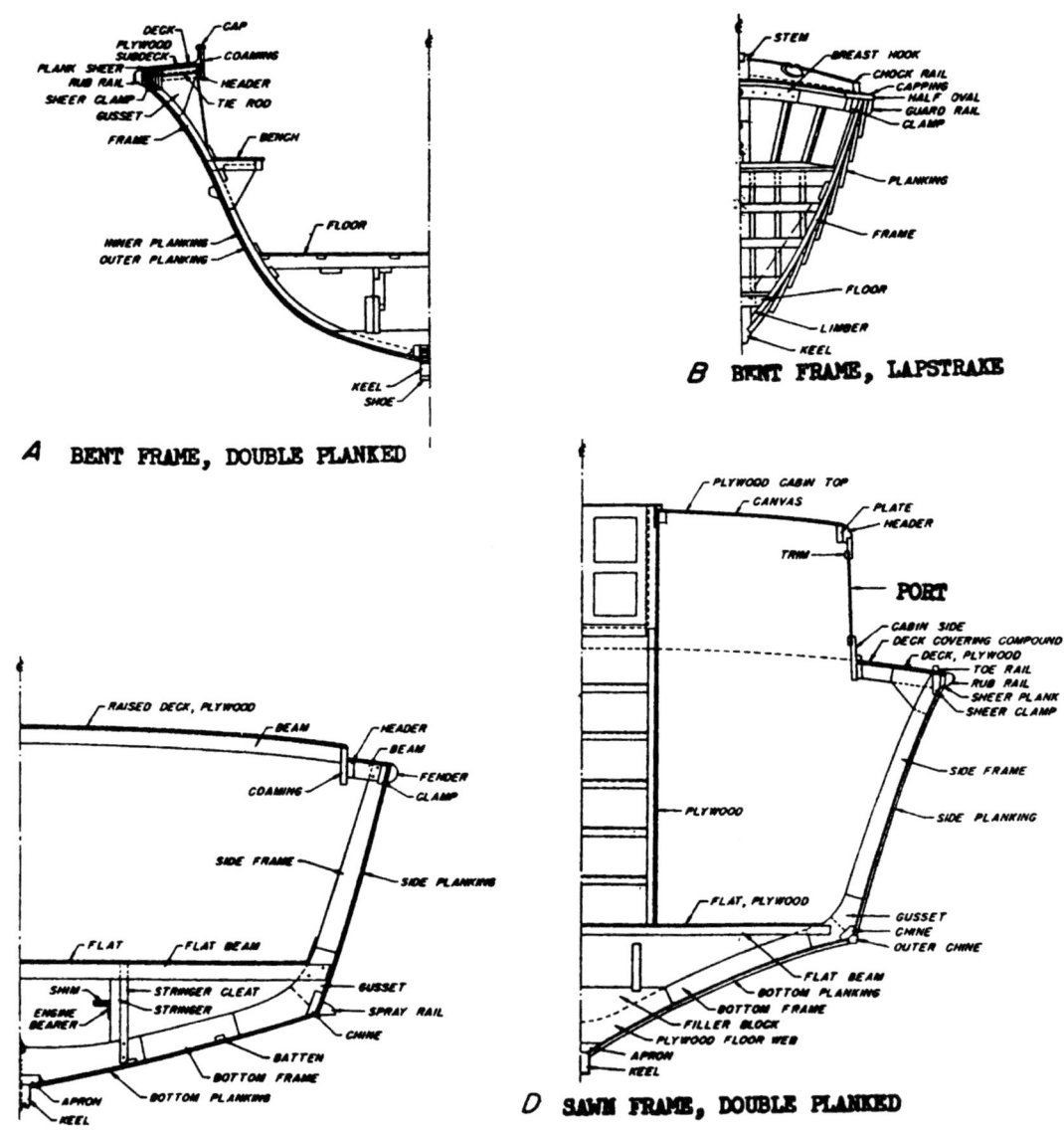

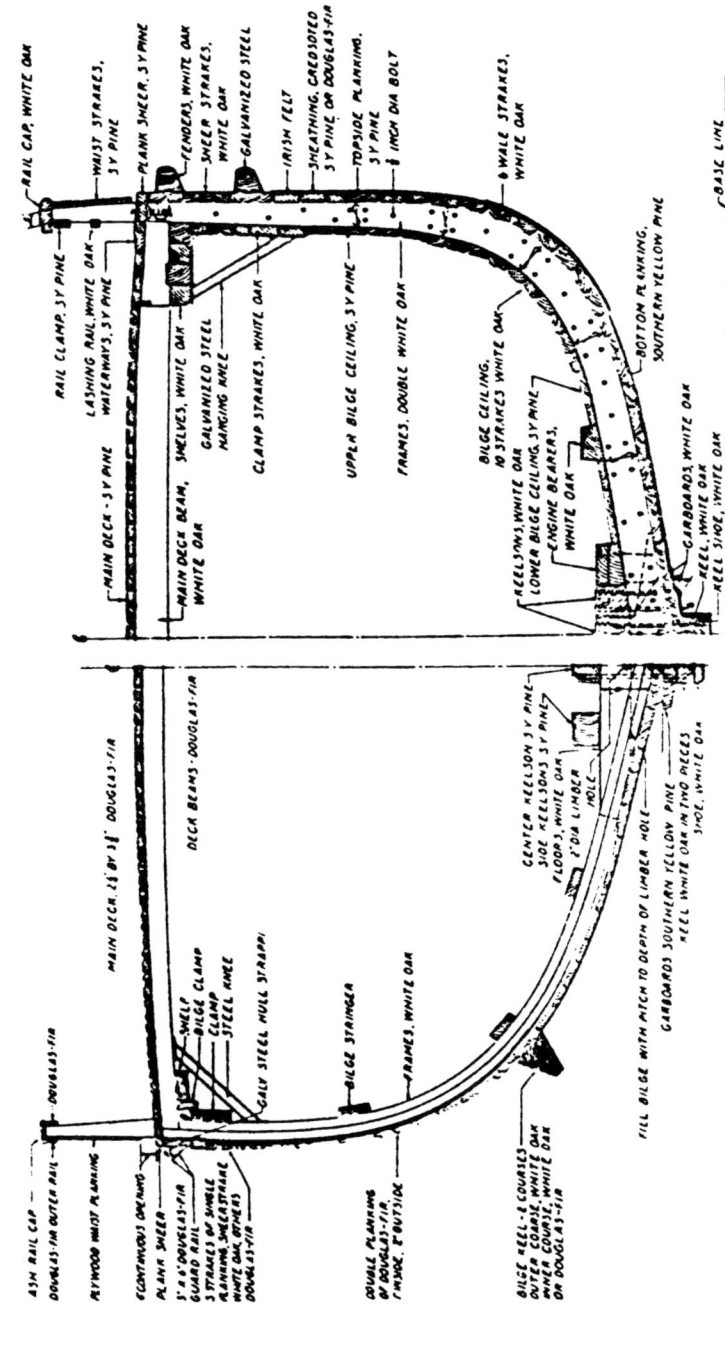

SECTIONS TYPICAL OF HEAVY CONSTRUCTION
LEFT - BENT FRAME
RIGHT - SAWN FRAME

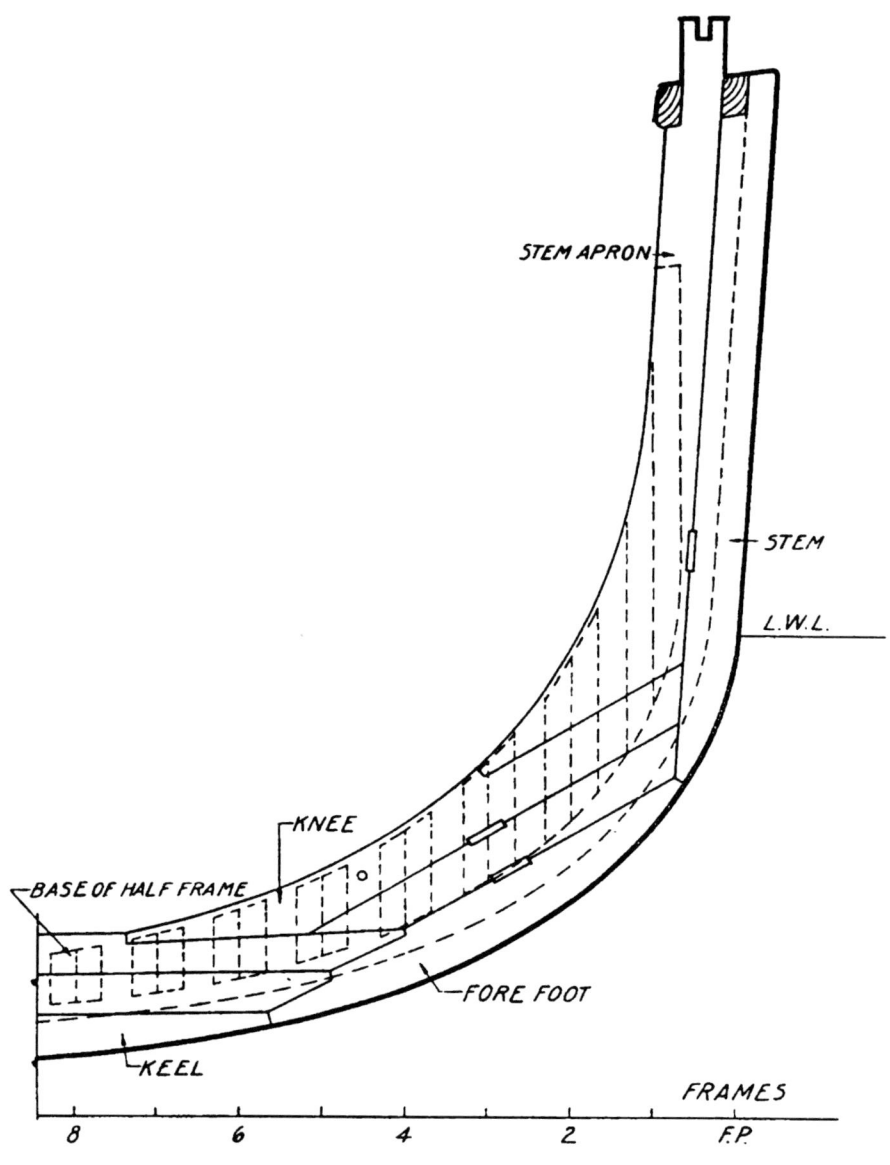

TYPICAL HEAVY STEM CONSTRUCTION

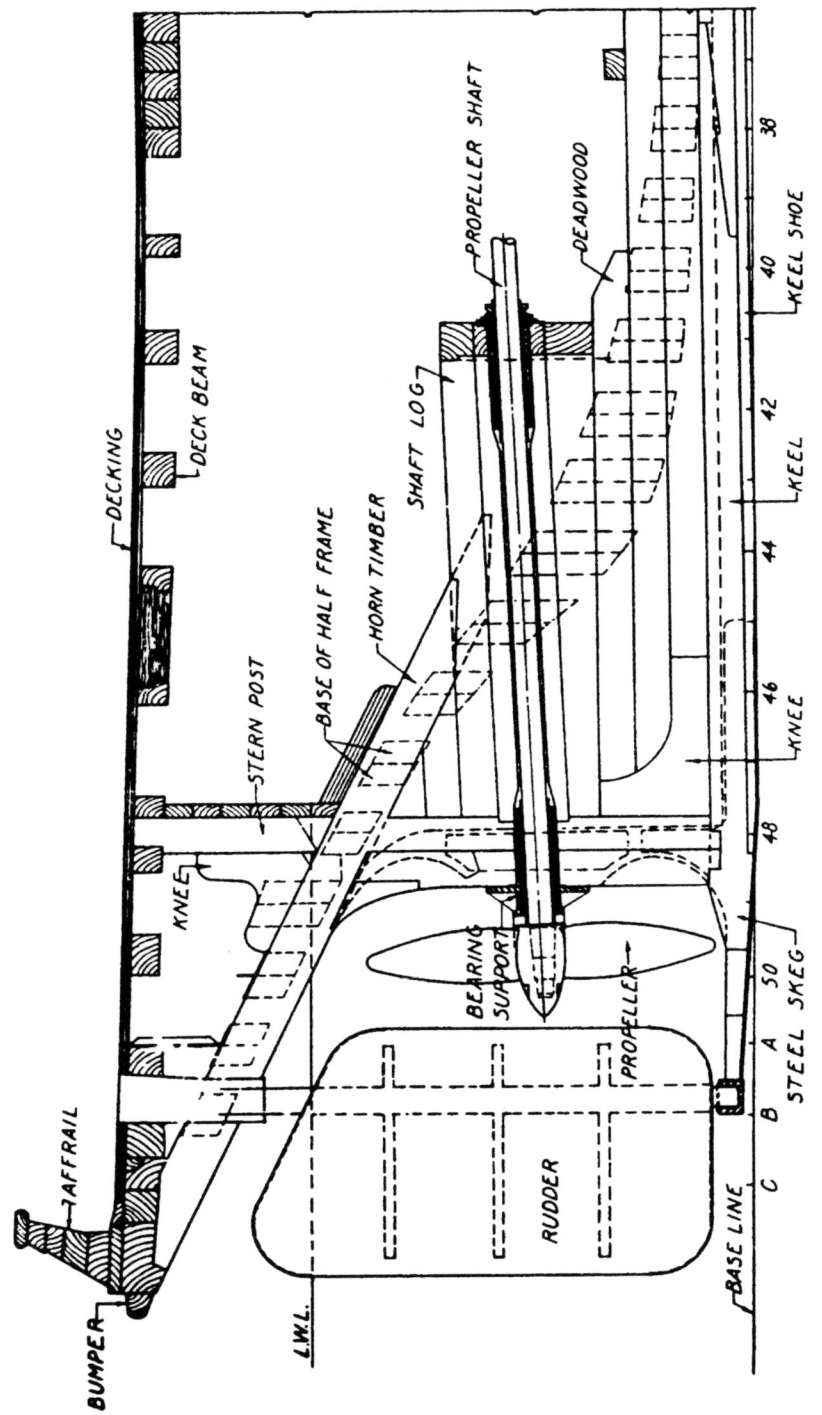

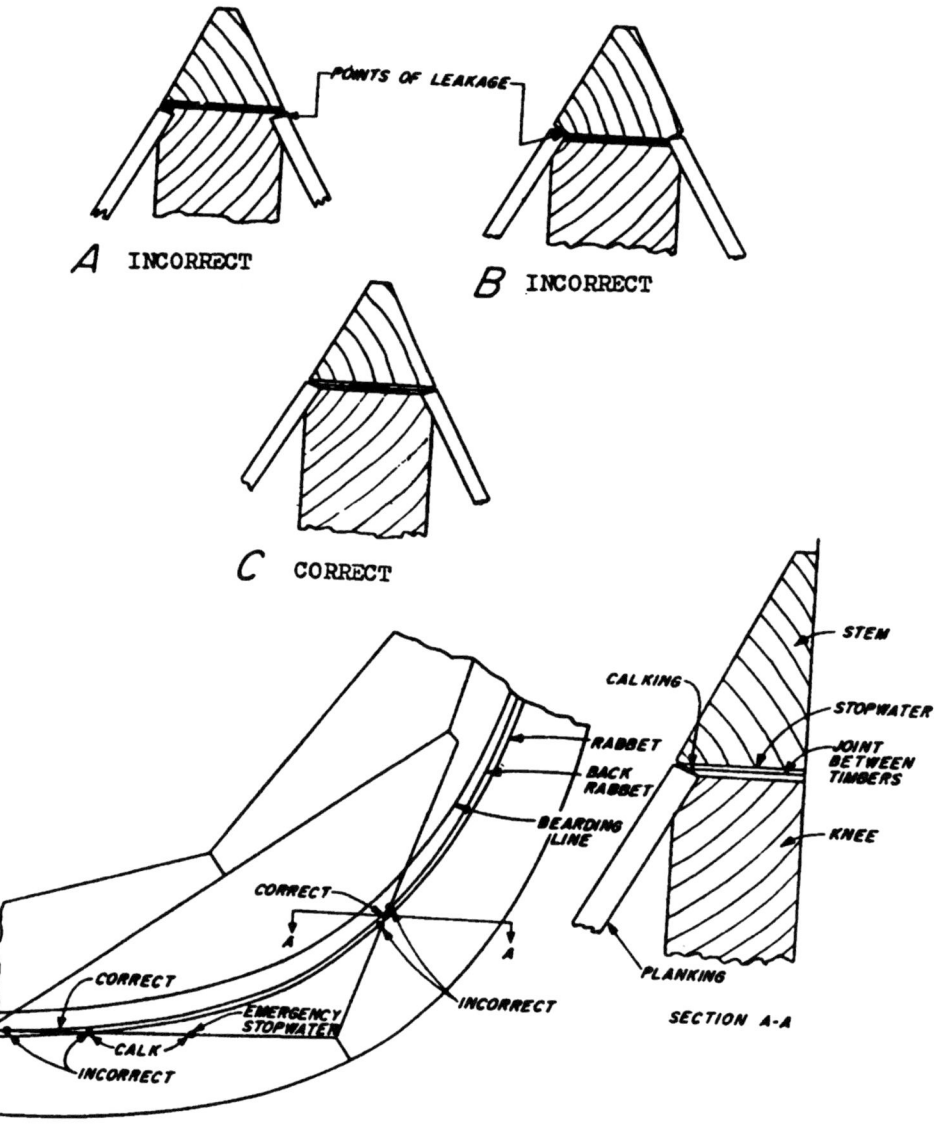

LOCATIONS OF STOPWATERS IN A STEM PIECE

VI. B. Glossary

Ashcroft - Construction - Double diagonal planking system with the planks of both skins raking in the same direction.

Backbone - The "spine" of the hull from which the frames radiate.

Back rabbet - Innermost angle or line of rabbet in which the garboard strake is set in the keel; any rabbet cut to receive planking at other than a right angle.

Ballast - Added weight either within or external to the hull added to improve the stability of a vessel or bring it down to its designed lines.

Bastard sawn - Hardwood lumber in which the annual rings make angles of 30° to 60° with the surface of the piece.

Batten - A thin flexible piece of wood.

Beam A structural member supporting a load applied transversely to it.

Beam - The width of a vessel. 2. The supporting structure for a deck.

Bearding line - The line formed by the intersection of the inside of the planking with the side or face of the keel.

Bending, steam - The process of forming curved wood members by steaming or boiling the wood and bending it to a form.

Bilge plank - A strengthening plank laid inside or outside of a vessel at the bilge's turn.

Binding strake - An extra thick strake of side or deck planking.

Buttock - That a part of a vessel's stern above her waterline which overhangs or lies abreast of the stern post; the counter.

Cant frames Frames whose plane of support is not perpendicular to the fore and aft line.

Capping - Fore and aft finished piece along the topsides of an open boat, often improperly termed gunwale; called a covering board, margin plank or plank sheer in a decked vessel.

Carlin - The fore and aft members of the deck framing system.

Carvel planked - Smooth skinned planking whose strakes run fore and aft.

Caulking (calking, (n)) - Cotton or other fiber driven into planking seams to make them watertight.

Ceiling - An inner skin of the hull often used to add strength in boats having sawn frames. In some cases the ceiling is not structural But merely serves to line the hull for decorative purposes or for ease in cleaning.

Check - A lengthwise separation of the wood that usually extends across the rings of annual growth and commonly results from stresses set up in wood during seasoning.

Chine - The line of intersection of the bottom with the side of the vessel.

Clamp - The fore and aft member at the sheer line of the vessel to which the deck beams usually fasten.

Clench planking - Lapstrake, in which the adjacent planks overlap like clapboards of a house.

Clinker built - See clench planking.

Coat, mast - A protective piece, usually canvas, covering the mast wedges where the mast enters the deck.

Cold bent (frames) - Frames which are bent on forms and after shaping are fitted to the vessel.

Cove line - A hollowed out decorative line found along the sheer of a boat.

Covering board - A plank used as a "washboard" or "plank sheer" along the outer edge of the deck. - see "capping".

Dead rise - The amount the bottom rises from keel to chine - most properly applied to "Vee" bottom construction but also used in reference to the rising bottom of round bottom boats.

Deadwood - The vertical structure built up from the keel to support the cant frames at the stern or stem.

Decay - The decomposition of wood substance by fungi.

1. (Advanced or typical) - The older stage of decay in which the destruction is readily recognized because the wood has become punky, soft and spongy, stringy, ringshaked, pitted or crumbly. Decided discoloration or bleaching of the rotted wood is often apparent.

2. (Incipient) - The early stage of decay that has not proceeded far enough to soften or otherwise perceptibly impair the hardness of the wood. It is usually accompanied by a slight discoloration or bleaching of the wood.

Diagonal planking - Planking laid on an angle to the keel.

Dry rot - A term loosely applied to any dry, crumbly rot but especially to that which, when in an advanced stage, permits the wood to be crushed easily to a dry powder. The term in actually a misnomer for any decay, since all fungi require considerable moisture for growth.

Dutchman - Wooden block or wedge used to fill the void in a badly made butt or joint; a graving piece or repairing patch in a deck; filler; shim; short plank.

Edged-grained lumber - Lumber that has been sawed so that the wide surfaces extend approximately at right angles to the annual growth rings. Lumber is considered edged grained when the rings form an angle of 45° to 90° with the wide surface of the piece.

Edging - Amount required to be cut away from the edge of a plank in fitting strakes.

Facing - Building one piece of timber on another for strength or finish purposes.

Flat-grained lumber - Lumber that has been sawed in a plan approximately perpendicular to a radius of the log. Lumber is considered flat grained when the annual growth rings make an angle of less thar 45° with the surface of the piece.

Floor - A transverse member being across the keel or a deep member of transverse framing.

Futtock - Curved parts or sections of transverse frames extending from the floor timbers to the top timbers.

Garboard - The strake nearest the keel.

Green - Freshly sawed lumber, or lumber that has received no intentional drying; unseasoned. The term does not apply to lumber that may have become completely wet through waterlogging.

Grub beam - A built up beam of short heavy timbers used to shape a round stern.

Heartwood - The wood extending from the pith to the sapwood, the cells of which no longer participate in the life processes of the tree. Heartwood may be infiltrated with gums, resins, and other materials that usually make it darker and more decay resistant than sapwood.

Horn timber - One or more timbers forming the main support for an overhanging stern and extending aft from the upper end of the stern post. Also used for timber connecting the shaft log and body post with the rudder post.

Horse (n) - The form upon which a small boat is built.

Horse (v) - To drive home, as to horse caulking.

Hot frame - A frame which, after being softened by heat, is pulled into shape as it is installed.

Joint - The junction of two pieces of wood or veneer.

> Butt joint - An end joint formed by abutting the squared ends of two pieces. Because of the inadequacy in strength of butt joints when glued, they are not generally used.

Edge joint - The place where two pieces of wood are joined together edge to edge, commonly by gluing. The joints may be made by gluing two squared edges as in a plain edge joint or by using machined joints of various kinds, such as tongued-and-grooved joints.

Scarf joint - An end joint formed by joining with glue and mechanical fastenings the ends of two pieces that have been tapered or beveled to form sloping plane surface, to the same length in both pieces. In some cases, a step or hook may be machined into the scarf to facilitate alignment of the two ends, in which case, the plane is discontinuous and the joint is known as a stepped or hooked scarf joint.

End joint - The place where two pieces of wood are joined together end to end, commonly by scarfing and gluing.

Lap joint - A joint made by placing one piece partly over another and bonding the overlapped portions.

Starved Joint - A glued joint that is poorly bonded because insufficient quantity of glue remained in the joint. Starved joints are caused by the use of excessive pressure or insufficient viscosity of the glue, or a combination of these, which result in the glue being forced out from between the surfaces to be joined.

King plank - The centerline plank of a deck.

> Knot - That portion of a branch or limb which has been surrounded by subsequent growth of the wood of the trunk or other portion of the tree. As a knot appears on the sawed surface, it is merely a section of the entire knot, its shape depending upon the direction of the cut.

Limber - A hole allowing the free passage of water from one area to another.

Molding - Measurement of a plank or timber from inboard to outboard, i.e., parallel to the plane in which the member lies; opposed to siding measured at right angles to such plane. Thus, the molding of a frame is measured in the thwartship direction while that of a stern piece is its cross sectional dimension fore and aft.

Nib - The squared off end of a tapered piece such as a scarf.

Partner - Stiffening or supporting pieces fitted in way of the passage of a mast through a deck.

Paying - Calking.

Pitch pocket - An opening extending parallel to the annual growth rings containing, or that has contained, pitch, either solid or liquid.

Plank sheer - see capping.

Preservative - Any substance that for a reasonable length of time is effective in preventing the development and action of wood-rotting fungi, borers of various kinds and harmful insects that deteriorate wood.

Prick post - An outer post supporting an outboard rudder.

Quartersawed lumber - Another term for edge-grained lumber.

Rabbet - A longitudinal channel or groove in a member which receives another piece to make a joint.

Ripped frame - A bent frame partially split longitudinally to make bending easier.

Rot - see decay.

Shake - A separation along the grain, the greater part of which occurs between the rings of annual growth.

Shelf - Line of timbers bridging and thus stiffening frames but chiefly for supporting the end of the deck beams.

Siding - see molding.

Spiling - The edge curve in a strake of planking.

Split - A lengthwise separation of the wood due to the tearing apart of the wood cells.

Stain - A discoloration in wood that may be caused by such diverse agencies as micro-organisms, metal, or chemicals. The term also applies to materials used to impart color in wood.

Stealer - In the shell planking toward the ends of a vessel a strake introduced as a single continuation of two tapering strakes.

Stopwater - A softwood piece driven across a scarf, as in the keel, to prevent seepage of water into the hull. Any contrivance to accomplish this purpose.

Strake - One of the rows or strips of planking constituting the surface of the hull.

Wane - Bark or lack of wood from any cause on edge or corner of a piece.

Warp - Any variation from a true or plane surface. Warp includes bow, crook, cup and twist or any combination thereof.

Weathering - The mechanical or chemical disintegration and discoloration of the surface of wood is caused by exposure to light, action of dust and sand carried by winds and alternate shrinking and swelling of the surface fibers with the variation in moisture content brought by changes in the weather. Weathering does not include decay.

Welt - A strip of wood fastened over a flush joint or seam for strengthening purposes. A seam batten.

VII. REFERENCES

The following recommended references should be of help to persons concerned with wooden boats.

Many of these publications contain additional lists of references which cover practically every facet of wood and wooden construction that might be of interest.

1. <u>Rules for the Construction and Classification of Wooden Ships</u>, American Bureau of Shipping, 45 Broad St., N.Y., N.Y.

2. <u>Naval Architecture of Small Craft</u> by D. Phillips Birt, Philosophical Library, Inc. 15 E. 40th Street, N.Y., N.Y. (Descriptive information on European small craft.)

3. <u>Boatbuilding</u> by Howard I. Chapell, W.W. Norton Co., N.Y, N.Y. (Comprehensive, well indexed and readable handbook of wood construction, though somewhat dated.)

4. <u>Fir Plywood Technical Data Handbook</u>, Douglas Fir Plywood Association, Tacoma, Wa. (Good reference book on fir plywood.)

5. <u>Rules for the Construction and Classification of Wood Yachts</u>, Lloyd's Register of Shipping, 71 Fenchurch Street, London, England

6. <u>National Design Specifications for Stress Grade Lumber and its Fastenings</u>, National Lumber Manufacturers Association, 1319 18th Street N.W., Washington, D.C. (Design information used for selecting fastenings and wood scantlings.)

7. <u>Wood: A Manual for its Use in Wooden Vessels</u>, Navy Department, Bureau of Ships, U.S. Government Printing Office, Washington, D.C. (Discussion of wood in small craft and ship construction.)

8. <u>Wood: A Manual for its Use as a Shipbuilding Material</u>, NAVSHIPS 250-336, U.S. Government Printing Office, Washington, D.C.
        Vol. I - Basic Wood Technology Applicable to
              Shipbuilding
        Vol. II - Techniques and Practices Applicable
              to Preservation and Storage.
        Vol. III - Technical Data Applicable to Boat and Ship
              Design
        Vol. IV - Techniques Applicable to Boat and
              Ship Construction

(Wood construction as it applies to the Navy. Good general reference.)

9.   Inspector's Handbook for Plastic Boats and Small Craft, NAVSHIPS 250-529-1

10.   Inspector's Handbook for Wooden Boats and Small Craft, NAVSHIPS 250-529-2, (Number 9 and 10 are pocket-sized outlines for the Navy Inspector. Useful for evaluating new boats.)

11.   Fabrication and Design of Glued Laminated Wood Structural Members, U.S. Department of Agriculture, Technical Bulletin No. 1069, U.S. Government Printing Office, Washington, D.C. (Production and use of plywood and wood laminate is covered thoroughly.)

12.   Wood Handbook (Handbook No. 72), U.S. Department of Agriculture, U.S. Government Printing Office, Washington, D.C. (Definitive treatment on wood, glues, fastenings, preservatives, etc. All phases of the production and use of wood.)

13.   Wood, Colors and Kinds (Handbook No. 101), U.S. Department of Agriculture, U.S. Government Printing Office, Washington, D.C. (American Wood - description of common species and color plates showing samples.)

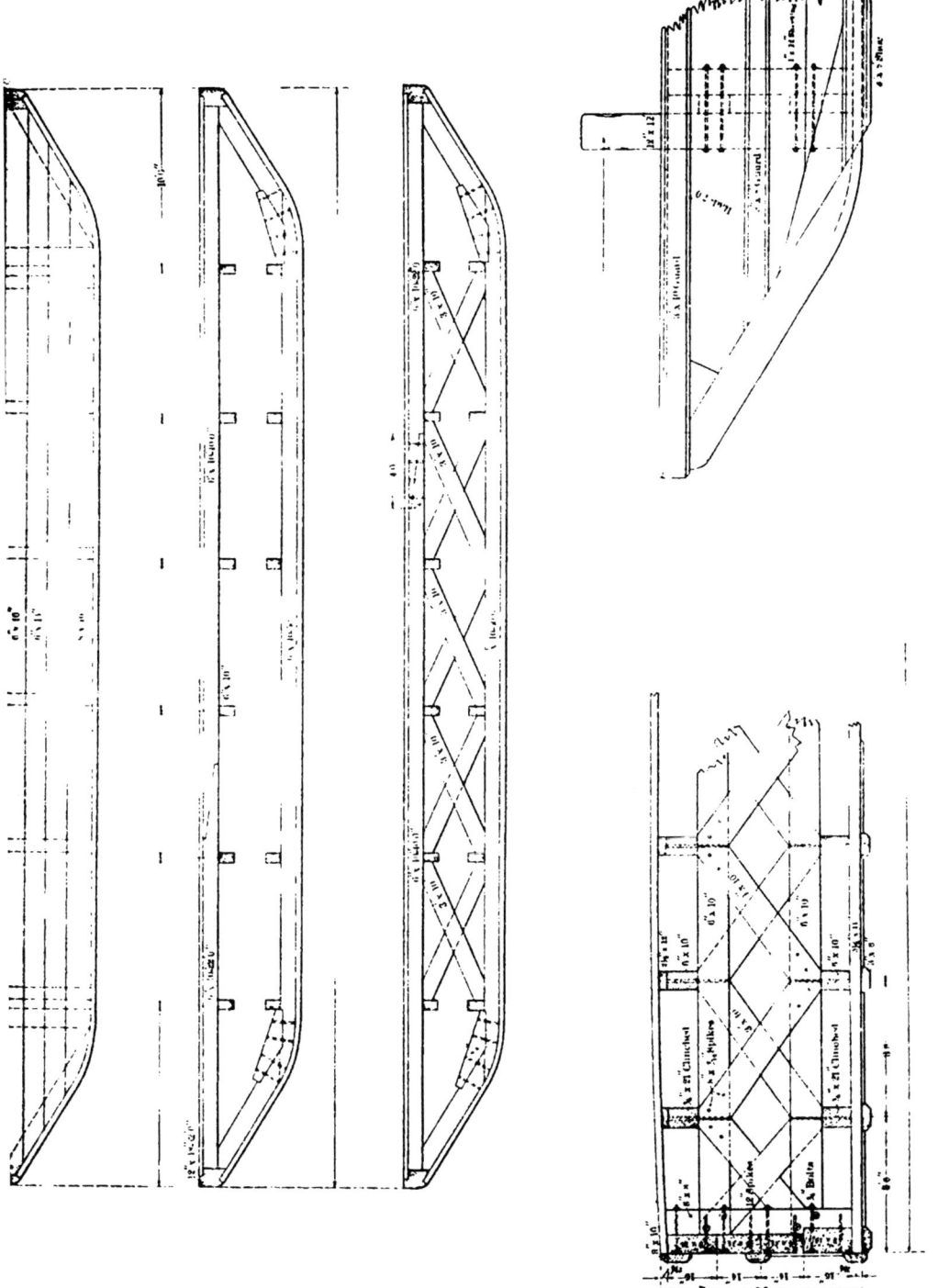

PLANS OF GAS TUG OHIO

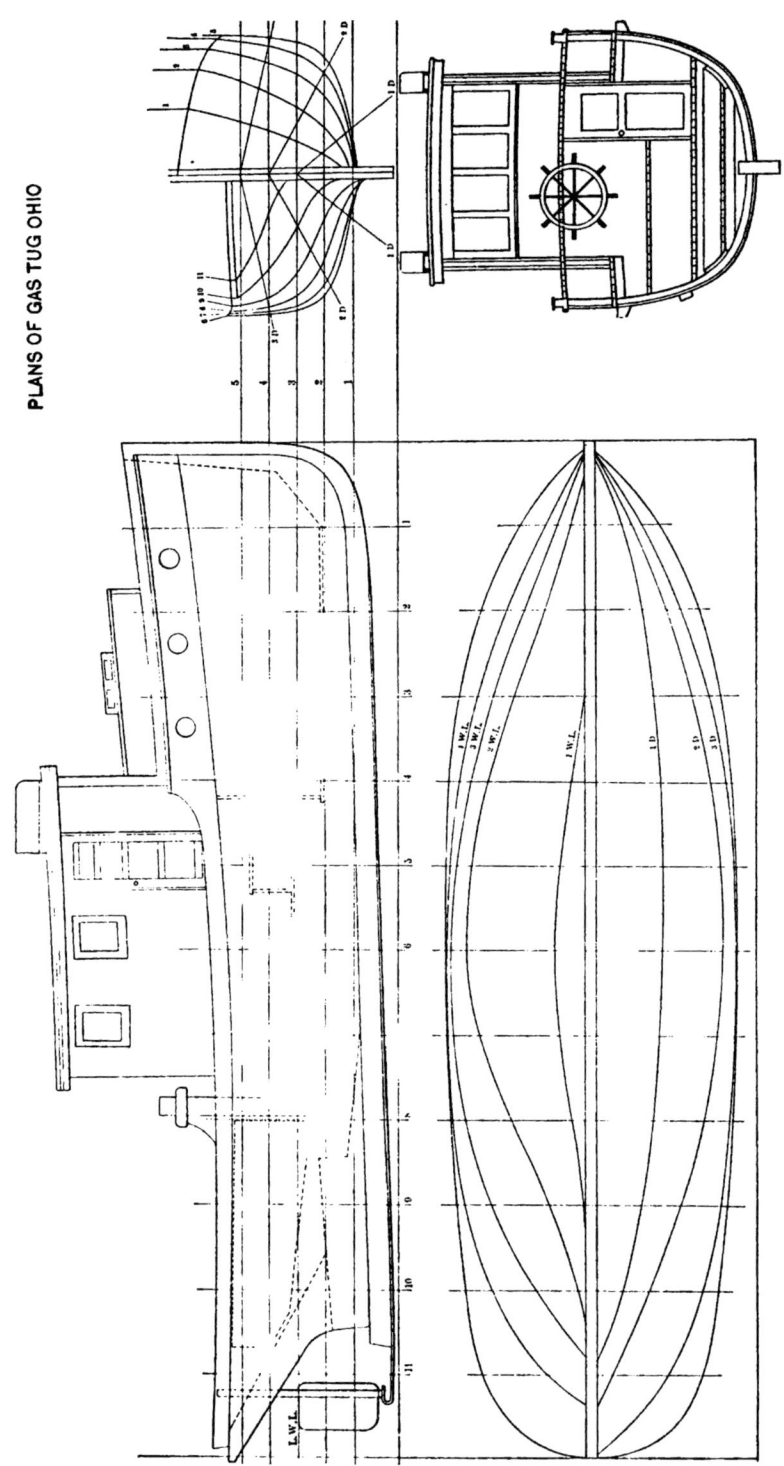